BRITAIN IN OLD PHOTOGRAPHS

WIMBLEDON

PATRICK LOOBEY
AND KEITH EVERY

The
History
Press

First published in 1995 by
Sutton Publishing Limited

Reprinted 2006

Reprinted in 2008 by
The Hiatory Press
The Mill, Brimscombe Port,
Stroud, Gloucestershire, GL5 2QG

British Library Cataloguing in Publication Data.
A catalogue record for this book is available from
the British Library.

ISBN 978-0-7509-0729-3

Typeset in 9/10 Sabon.
Typesetting and origination by
Sutton Publishing Limited.
Printed and bound in England.

Keith Every was born in 1944 and lived in Putney until moving to Wimbledon in 1955. He worked in the printing trade for thirty-two years and has recently started his own garden maintenance business. The chance find of some old postcards of Wimbledon at an antiques fair some ten years ago kindled a passion for Edwardian picture postcards. His collection of approximately 4,000 views, mainly of Wimbledon and Raynes Park, also includes the surrounding areas.

Patrick Loobey was born in 1947 and had lived in Balham, Putney, Southfields and Streatham – all within the Borough of Wandsworth. He joined the Wandsworth Historical Society (founded in 1953) in 1969 and had served on its archaeological, publishing and management committees, being chairman of the society from 1991 to 1994. He had a wide-ranging collection of approximately 20,000 Edwardian postcards of Wandsworth borough and south-west London, encompassing many local roads and subjects.

The captions to the photographs in this book are but a brief glimpse into the varied and complex history of the area. For those seeking further information, the Wimbledon Society (formerly the John Evelyn Society) has published many booklets on the area's history and maintains a museum and archive on the Ridgway (open Saturdays). The Wandsworth Historical Society has also published histories that cover part of Wimbledon's past – namely Wimbledon Common, Southfields and Wimbledon Park. It can be contacted via the Wandsworth Museum. The Lawn Tennis Museum, Church Road, has an extensive library that can be consulted by appointment. The Windmill Museum on Wimbledon Common is open during the summer on Saturdays. The reference libraries at Hill Road, Wimbledon and at Lavender Hill, Battersea have early newspapers, deeds, directories, maps and parish records which are made available to those wishing to research names, dates and addresses of families or business concerns.

Thanks must go to my sister Doreen Loobey, who was enlisted to plough through local directories in the reference library.

Photograph credits (page numbers: T = top, L = lower):
4, 5, 7, 8L, 12T, 18L, 20L, 21T, 22L, 23T, 25L, 27T, 29T, 30, 31T, 32T, 33T, 35, 36, 37, 38L, 40T, 43, 46, 47L, 48T, 50, 51, 52, 53T, 54T, 55L, 57L, 62T, 66, 71T, 73, 74T, 77L, 79L, 80, 82L, 83, 84T, 87T, 88L, 93L, 94T, 97, 99T, 100, 105, 108T, 113T, 115L, 116T, 117T, 123T, 124, 125L, 126, all copyright P.J. Loobey.
All others copyright Keith Every.

Contents

The windmill, Wimbledon, *c.* 1922. Besides the tennis tournaments, the windmill is the most recognizable symbol of Wimbledon.

Introduction

The scenes within these pages illustrate the gradual change from a rural Wimbledon with elegant eighteenth-century houses to the modern London suburb of today.

Wimbledon Common has seen much activity – the early military reviews, mustering of volunteers, pistol duels, meetings of the National Rifle Association. Then it was used as a training camp and airfield during the First World War. The greatest threat was in the 1860s when Earl Spencer wanted to enclose and develop the common, but it was saved in 1871 and now resounds to nothing more serious than flying golf-balls or dogs being exercised.

The coming of the railway in 1838 was an impetus to development; John Beaumont in the Wimbledon Park area and the British Land Co. bought up huge tracts of land, and in the 1860s they laid down the roads which were subsequently built on.

The population in 1861 of 4,644 had increased to 55,000 by 1911, bringing the need for churches, schools, small-scale industry and shops to service the greater numbers.

Cottenham Park caught the development fever after the opening of Raynes Park station in 1871, but it was not until after the First World War that the West Barnes district was covered with new housing and schools.

Although damage during the Second World War was not severe, 600 houses were totally destroyed, as the odd inconsistencies in architectural style will testify. Many of the large Victorian houses were removed during the 1960s and replaced by blocks of flats. The centre of the town was transformed in the 1980s, with towering office blocks and shops altering the skyline, but then the history of the area has been one of constant change.

The name Wimbledon is famous all over the world because of the tennis championships which are held here every year. But the area is more varied and distinctive in character then its international reputation might suggest. This book aims to record the architecture of Wimbledon and scenes from local life in order to give a vivid impression of the Wimbledon district over the last 100 years.

Wimbledon High Street, *c*. 1907. Note how the lady is guarding her fair skin against any risk of a sun tan.

Wimbledon Town Hall, *c*. 1933. This was the centre of civic pride of the Borough of Wimbledon from 1931 to 1965.

Section One

WIMBLEDON VILLAGE

Wimbledon, c. 1920. The houses on Parkside and Parkside Gardens can be seen with the village beyond. The triangle at the edge of the common is yet to receive the war memorial.

Wimbledon, *c.* 1920. Rushmere pond and the houses on the Green occupy the lower half, with the High Street just above the Green. The number of trees that appear among the houses is surprising.

Wimbledon, *c.* 1920. Rushmere pond is at the top left. King's College School is visible in the lower part of the picture, with the large houses on Southside facing the common. The smaller cottages at Crooked Billet can just be seen at lower left.

The High Street in 1907. The horse-drawn bus to Putney is being diverted to the left while the road is worked on. The turreted building at No. 54 High Street was the grocers and post office of T.G. Mason which in 1920 still had nine collections a day. No. 37 on the left was shared between T. Gibbard & Sons decorators and water engineers and W. Calloway & Sons cowkeepers and dairymen.

The Rose and Crown public house, *c.* 1933. It probably dates back to at least 1659 when it was just called The Rose, possibly a result of the recent civil war. The writer Swinburne would often walk from his home in Putney to the pub and relax within a private room where his favourite chair still resides.

The High Street, *c*. 1933. Berry's at No. 65 on the right was offering lock-up garages for rent at *7s 6d* per week. This was previously the dining rooms of Mr Henry Duck. Sigger & Sons bootmakers occupied No. 61, beyond the tobacconist's, for some years.

The High Street, *c*. 1925. The Dog and Fox public house on the right is first mentioned in 1617 and is the oldest Wimbledon inn still in use, although the present building dates from 1869. The tower on the left, built in 1890, housed the local fire engine until the new fire station in Queen's Road opened in 1904. Being the heart of the village, the High Street has the greatest number of pubs. Visible on the left is The Brewery Tap.

The High Street, *c*. 1950. It still had a number of family-owned shops such as Higgins butcher's and Davies chemist's on the corner of Church Road.

The High Street, *c*. 1907. The row of shops seen in the 1950 view had not yet been built and trees still occupied the site on the right beyond the horse-drawn bus. T. Shaw's small shop on the left offered a picture framing and book binding service and also supplied a range of stationery.

The High Street at the junction with the Ridgway in 1907. It still had the air of a rural village. At No. 7 on the left is A.J. Smith wine and spirit merchant, and next door at No. 8 is Walker's dairy. The decorators are using extra-long ladders to paint the shop front; scaffolding would be used today.

The Ridgway, c. 1907. The interesting shopping parade includes Cadman & Co. chemist's, Norman Jenkins stationer, Arthur Cockle grocer and post office at Nos 75–7, and further along was Francis Randall baker's and William Stevens butcher's.

The Swan public house on the Ridgway in 1913. Mr John Daniel Maier was publican. The public house was situated alongside the stables of Johnson & Wells jobmasters, who by 1913 had added the term 'garage' to the firm's description. The Ridgway stables in 1995 operate from the same premises.

The Ridgway, c. 1933. Compare this scene with the earlier picture. The spelling of this roadway without an 'e' is peculiar to Wimbledon.

The raised footpath on Wimbledon Hill, *c.* 1910. It was sometimes called The Lover's Walk.

Section Two

WIMBLEDON TOWN CENTRE

Central Wimbledon from the air, c. 1920. The railway station, with the wider carriageway entrance, is in the middle of this view with the Broadway on the top right. Queen's Road, parallel to the railway, is on the top left.

Woodside Road from the hill during a winter, *c.* 1910. Four men are shovelling snow onto carts for disposal. Local authorities would often use the unemployed to clear snow from the streets and pavements. The expense of this operation in January 1927 was of much local interest and became a leading subject in the local papers.

Hill Road near the corner of Woodside Road, *c.* 1910. On the left is the business of David Stewart Thompson & Sons nurserymen, and on the corner of Alwyn Road is his son's premises, Robert John Thompson FRIBA architect.

Hill Road, *c.* 1920. Two No. 70 general omnibuses en route from Putney Bridge to Merton Park are passing each other. On the right is H.E. Randall high-class bootmaker, and on the corner of Alwyn Road is the shop of Edward Vergette costumier.

Hill Road in 1907. A new electric tram is en route to Summerstown. The library on the corner of Compton Road was erected in 1886–7 to the designs of Messrs Potts, Sulman and Hemmings, at the estimated cost of £2,500; it opened in 1887. It was enlarged in 1902 at a cost of £3,000. 1995 also saw further alterations and improvements.

The junction of Hill Road and Worple Road, *c.* 1920. The Alexandra public house, built in 1876, is visible on the left and Ely's store on the right. During the 1980s and '90s the area on the right down to the railway has been rebuilt and is unrecognizable from this scene.

Ely's department store in 1912. Joseph Ely built the store in the grounds of his own house in about 1886. The family had started their draper's and outfitter's store in Alexandra Road ten years earlier. The window display seen here must have taken many hours to prepare.

Worple Road, after May 1907. The new trams seen alongside Ely's store had only been introduced and allowed to travel as far as Hill Road from 2 May 1907. The full system was not working for some months which led to frustration and ribald comments from the locals.

The Odeon cinema in Worple Road, c. 1945. It opened on 20 April 1936 and seated 1,501. The last film was shown on 20 November 1960 and the cinema was subsequently demolished.

Worple Road in 1907. An early motor car is scorching along at the speed limit – in most towns of 10 m.p.h. Motor traffic was limited until the 1920s and most deliveries were still by horse and cart, as seen here with the delivery vehicle from Pratt's department store of Streatham. In the background is the Methodist church, erected in 1886 with seating for 600. Due to structural problems the church was demolished and the congregation transferred to the Raynes Park Methodist Church.

Worple Road in 1907. Hampton Court is the destination for this tram. The trees seen here were survivors from the period before development took place.

Worple Road in 1907. The tram was king of the road for almost thirty years; as we can see here, it had little competition. Open trams were uncomfortable in rain and winter and within a few years were all given top deck roofs.

Worple Road, c. 1920. The photographer R.J. Johns of Longley Road, Tooting has managed to capture an almost deserted scene. Many of the properties had been built by 1890. The road's name was for several centuries The Upper Worple Way, when it was just a track between the ploughed fields.

Hill Road, *c.* 1910. Trim's printing works are visible on the right where many of the local directories and some of these postcard views were printed. Ely's tailors and outfitters were still operating from premises at No. 13 at the corner of Alexandra Road.

The junction of Hill Road and St George's Road in 1907. The London and County Bank building survived until 1994 when it was demolished. We must be grateful to Mr Hutchinson for taking many of these views and reproducing them as postcards in 1907 and 1908.

The bottom of Hill Road opposite the station, *c.* 1926. With the station restaurant and office of J. Price coal and coke merchants on the right, the scene hardly differs from the one below except for the motive power and the addition of bitumen tarmac to the road surface.

The same scene, *c.* 1900.

Hill Road, Christmas 1908. Shopping districts during the Edwardian era vied with each other to attract shoppers to their area, and here we see Hill Road by the Alexandra public house and also by the station approach, welcoming visitors with flags and bunting in abundance.

Tram negotiating the turn into St George's Road, *c.* 1907. The tram lines were laid in Wimbledon during 1906 but the Council would not allow the London United Tramway Co. to use them until all the road widenings and alterations were completed; the Summerstown route was eventually opened on 27 June 1907. This picture was taken in the first months of operation. The speed restriction demanded by Wimbledon Council on the tramways was 4 m.p.h. on curves.

St George's Road at the corner of Hill Road in 1907. The tram has a full complement of passengers on the journey to Hampton Court. The sign above the shop on the left is offering 'a good dinner for 6*d*'.

The Broadway opposite the station, *c*. 1912. A soon-to-be-replaced horse-drawn bus is trundling past. Hartfield Road is off to the right with The Prince of Wales public house, a late Victorian addition, in its prominent position on the corner.

The railway station, *c*. 1908. It was opened in 1838 when the London and South West Railway Co. opened its line from Nine Elms to Southampton. Other companies requiring extra platforms were the London Brighton and South Coast Railway in 1855 and the District Railway in 1889. The present station entrance was built by Southern Railways in 1929. The yard on the left had a number of coal company offices and also Hawes & Co. depository, seen here with the furniture vans outside.

The Broadway in 1907. One of the new trams is crossing the rail bridge by the station entrance. The maximum permitted speed for trams on the bridge was 8 m.p.h. Hartfield Road is on the left.

The Broadway, c. 1912. The old town hall is on the right and the station entrance beyond the tram. The flower seller standing on the roadside would have a difficult job today.

The Broadway by the town hall, *c.* 1936. An ex-London United Tramways trolleybus, nicknamed 'diddlers', is awaiting passengers. The trolleybuses were introduced in 1931 and taken over by the London Passenger Transport Board in 1933 when many of the passenger transport firms were amalgamated. A London County Council tram, advertising Black and White Whiskey, can be seen on the left; these arrived in May 1926 when through-running was introduced from Tooting – the LCC and LUT lines in Tooting High Street were not connected before then.

The town hall, *c.* 1926. The building of the earlier town hall was erected in 1878 for use as administrative offices for the the local board of health, becoming the town hall in 1905 when Wimbledon gained its borough charter.

The new town hall after it was opened in November 1931. With the amalgamation of Wimbledon and Merton boroughs in 1965 and the subsequent building of Crown House in Morden as new council headquarters, the town hall was declared redundant in 1985. During the early 1990s it was converted into offices associated with the Centre Court shopping development.

Queen's Road, c. 1909. The photographer's shop of Collins & Kew is on the right; they were portrait photographers who also produced some of the scenes in this book. On the left is the Baptist chapel with seating for 1,000 people, and next door is the fire station.

The fire station, Queen's Road, *c.* 1909. It was built in 1904 as a replacement for the smaller station in the High Street opposite the Dog and Fox public house. The horse-drawn steam pumps were replaced by motor fire engines in 1913. A new fire station was built on the Kingston Road during the late 1980s, and the 1904 station converted into a shop as part of the Centre Court shopping development.

The Broadway shops packed with goods for sale, *c.* 1914. John Best, pork and beef butcher, occupies the shop on the right; beyond that, 'high class teeth' can be purchased from Wilson's dental surgery.

The Broadway in 1950. The Home & Colonial stores on the left provided the daily provisions for many local households. Parking restrictions were not yet in operation although no driver could stop within the metal studs set in the roadway about twenty yards either side of the pedestrian crossing. In the far distance is the Odeon cinema, opened in 1933 as the Regal. It was renamed the Gaumont in 1949 and given its present name in 1962 after the Odeon in Worple Road closed.

A view of the Broadway taken from the top of the theatre, *c.* 1910. All of the shop blinds are down to protect the goods on display from sunlight discolouration.

The Broadway, *c.* 1926. Wimbledon theatre is a prominent landmark. Among the shops here was that of W.J. Harris & Co., whose prams could be purchased for under £5.

Merton Road in 1907. It was later renamed the Broadway. Beyond the tram are the two large houses soon to make way for Wimbledon theatre, which opened in 1910.

The Broadway, *c.* 1914. Visible is the parade of shops erected since the previous photograph was taken. Among them can be seen the archway entrance to the King's Palace cinema which opened in October 1910. This parade of shops and the cinema were demolished 1993–4 for redevelopment.

Looking towards the corner of the Broadway and Merton Road from Latimer Road, *c.* 1933. St Winifred's Roman Catholic Church is to the left and on the far corner at No. 113 Merton Road is Owen Bros cash grocers and post office, which had nine collections weekdays from 8.40 a.m. to 10.30 p.m. and two on Sundays.

The corner of Merton Road and Quicks Road, *c.* 1908. A Summerstown-bound tram is negotiating the single line working in this narrow stretch of road. A set of stop-and-go traffic lights for trams were in operation on the corner of Pelham Road until 1951 when diesel buses took over the service.

Section Three

MERTON

High Street, Colliers Wood, c. 1930. The Royal Standard public house is on the left. The City and South London Railway Co. extended the underground railway from Clapham to Morden between 1923 and 1926, finally opening in December 1926. Many of the stations on this stretch of the Northern Line were built to a similar design by Charles Holden, who also designed the London Transport logo of a circle and bar.

The Royal Six Bells public house in High Street, Colliers Wood, *c.* 1922. This is the point where the old line of the Roman Stane ('stane' = stone) street from Chichester to London is lost until it reappears in Morden. The modern road follows the line almost without deviation from London Bridge to this vicinity.

The King's Head public house at 18 High Street, Merton, *c.* 1908. Situated almost opposite the now-demolished twelfth-century Merton priory, it is just possible that the date of 1496 proclaimed for the pub could be correct. Young & *Co.* substantially rebuilt and enlarged the pub in 1931.

High Street, Merton. The view above from *c.* 1907 shows the position of the King's Head public house by the River Wandle. The property for sale to the right was soon to be bought by the London General Omnibus Co. for use as a bus garage, which is seen below in the mid-1920s. It is still in use.

Merton High Street near the junction with Haydon's Road, *c.* 1920. On the outside wall of the Nelson public house is a beautiful coloured tile panel of the HMS *Victory*, Admiral Nelson's flagship at the battle of Trafalgar in 1805.

Merton High Street where it joins Merton Road, *c.* 1922. The cottages at Eliza Place on the right were soon to be demolished for South Wimbledon tube station. The Horse and Groom public house on the right is still serving up cups of cheer.

Section Four

WIMBLEDON
COMMON

Rushmere pond on the common, c. 1925. It was created by the removal of gravel for repairing local roads during the medieval era. The name probably derives from rushes or reeds that grew around the pond.

Caesar's Well, *c.* 1912. This is the site of a natural spring but the water now appears from a pipe a few yards from the well. Sir Henry Peek MP had the granite wall installed around the well in 1872 and the pine trees were planted soon after. The Roman Emperor Julius Caesar had no connection with the well or with Caesar's Camp, the iron age fort to the south.

The windmill, *c.* 1925. It was built in 1817 by a carpenter from Roehampton and stopped grinding corn in 1864. Lord Baden-Powell wrote *Scouting for Boys* here in 1907–8 and the mill was the headquarters for the National Rifle Association meetings held on the common from 1860 to 1889 when they moved the shoots to Bisley. During the First World War an emergency airfield was laid out nearby, and after landing the pilot was instructed 'to proceed to No. 1 The Windmill for further orders'. The Windmill Museum was opened in 1976 to document the history of windmills.

Queensmere pond in 1910. The pond was created in 1887 by damming up a small stream across a small valley on the west side of the common to commemorate Queen Victoria's diamond jubilee. A small rowing boat kept for rescues can be seen in this scene. Many of the National Rifle Association target butts can still be traced hereabouts.

The fountain on Parkside opposite Parkside Avenue, c. 1908. It was the gift of Robert Hanbury MP, and the horse trough was provided by the Metropolitan Fountain Association and erected by Wills Bros. Among the biblical quotes inscribed on the base is 'the fear of the lord is a fountain of life'. An unusual cast-iron Ordnance Survey benchmark is set in the pavement on Parkside opposite the fountain.

Warren Farm to the west of the windmill in 1910. The farm survived until the Second World War when it was damaged on several occasions; the remains were demolished at war's end. As seen in this view, the wooded area was popular for picnics.

Kingsmere pond, *c*. 1925. The pond is on the Putney side of the parish boundary which runs across the common from Tibbet's Corner to the windmill. The Kingston Road (A3) is on the left. The pond, created from gravel working, was a popular spot for summer picnics and paddling until the Tibbet's Corner underpass and road widening to six lanes took place in 1970, making it difficult for traffic to stop here.

Skating on Kingsmere pond during wintertime, *c.* 1910.

Kingsmere pond almost swamped by the numbers of children during a glorious Edwardian summer, *c.* 1910.

Beverley Brook near the Kingston Road in 1906. The stream is first mentioned in Saxon boundary charters and probably gets its name from beavers that once lived here. Although not a fast flowing river, during the medieval period a small mill probably operated to the west of Warren Farm at a place on the stream called Mill Corner.

Canteen on the common, 1916. The Young Men's Christian Association set up a rest room and canteen as a quiet retreat from the wartime duty of guarding London's approaches and the arduous training routine. Private and commercial organizations supplied the rest room canteens up to 1921 when the government founded the Navy, Army and Air Force Institutes (NAAFI).

Barrack blocks on the common, 1919. During the First World War 5,000 troops were billeted on the common and housed in these wooden barrack blocks during their training before being shipped overseas. The camp was built in 1916 and removed in 1920.

Troops of No. 4 Company 2nd Battalion of the Honourable Artillery Company (infantry) parading on the common near Parkside, June 1916.

The war memorial, *c.* 1922. Situated on Parkside at the head of the common, the memorial was unveiled on 1 November 1921 by Sir Joseph Hood, MP for Wimbledon. Personal family tributes, as seen in this picture, were heaped around the monument each November well into the 1920s, in memory of the 1,400 from Wimbledon who did not return from the First World War.

A Sunday school outing to the common, *c.* 1908, by members from Emmanuel Chapel based on the Ridgway.

Memorial stone set up near the site of the training camp not far from the Queen's Butt, *c.* 1930. The inscription is 'To the memory of all ranks of the reserve battalions of the King's Royal Rifle Corps who trained here and afterwards gave their lives for King and Country 1916–18'.

Hanford Row, *c*. 1910. It was built in 1770 on Westside next to Cannizaro House and the cottages survive almost unaltered.

Clifton House, 10 Southside, *c*. 1908. The house stood overlooking the common near Lauriston Road and before the First World War was the home of William Augustus Churchill. The house was badly damaged in a tip-and-run raid on 19 September 1944.

The High Street from Southside with the Green on the left and Lingfield Road to the right, *c.* 1908.

The Keir on Westside near Camp Road, *c.* 1910. It was the home of William Benson who died here in 1754. He was made surveyor-general of the Board of Works succeeding Sir Christopher Wren; he was also a great patron of literary men and erected a monument to John Milton in Westminster Abbey. The house was converted into flats in 1932.

The Crooked Billet, *c.* 1922. The Crooked Billet public house (on the extreme left) is first mentioned in 1509 as a brewery and inn, and it gave its name to the small row of cottages on either side of it. Here we see a sign writer repainting the pub sign for the Hand in Hand public house in the background. This was originally a bakehouse owned by a member of the Watney brewing family; it did not become a beer house until 1877.

The Fox and Grapes public house on Camp Road, near Westside, in 1908. It has not changed since this photograph was taken; the tiny alleyway by the pub is called West Court.

Section Five

WIMBLEDON PARK
& TENNIS

*Wimbledon Park Road, c. 1908. After the tennis tournaments came to the area in 1922 the
road was renamed Church Road. The view looks towards Southfields with the Wimbledon
Park lake and golf club house to the right. The park was formed from 1765 by John Spencer,
lord of the manor of Wimbledon, who bought 247 acres of land. It was landscaped by
Capability Brown, and the lake that he created is still the focus of the park.*

Wimbledon Park as seen from Victoria Road, *c.* 1908. Wimbledon Park Road (Church Road) is to the left and on the brow of the hill is St Mary's Parish Church. It was not until 1922 that the All England tennis grounds were built in the field in view.

Wimbledon Park lake as seen from Albert Road, *c.* 1910. Wimbledon Park Road (Church Road) can be seen at the bottom of the slope; the white fencing was to prevent any animals from straying.

Wimbledon Park lake, c. 1910. The grounds were bought by the Council for £121,000 in 1914, to save them from housing development, although several acres to the south of Home Park Road were sold separately after the First World War.

The golf course, *c*. 1922. The grass is being cut by a horse-drawn mower. The golf club was founded in 1899 and has an eighteen-hole course which is still a popular venue.

The tennis courts, *c*. 1930. The Corporation installed several sporting facilities within the park; the twenty tennis courts are well used each summer. The club house was destroyed by a V1 flying bomb in 1944 and subsequently rebuilt.

Families using the park for summer relaxation and picnics, *c.* 1925. This is probably the area south of Home Park Road sold in 1925 by the Council for housing development.

The Wimbledon tennis championships, as seen from the air, *c.* 1950. It entails two weeks of chaos for the residents of Southfields every June. The 1922 centre court stands out well, as does Church Road separating the courts from the park.

View from the centre court in the 1950s.

The buffet in the 1950s. The tennis championships have been famous for the quantities of strawberries and cream consumed each year. In the 1950s the buffet was a simple affair for light refreshments; it is still called the tea lawn, although it was paved over in the 1980s.

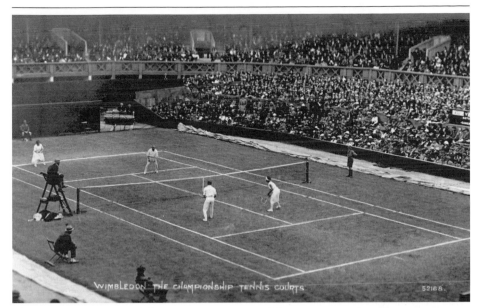

The centre court, 1923. The new centre court, with concrete stands and superstructure, was ready for the 1922 championships. Here we have a mixed doubles match featuring the French player Suzanne Lenglen.

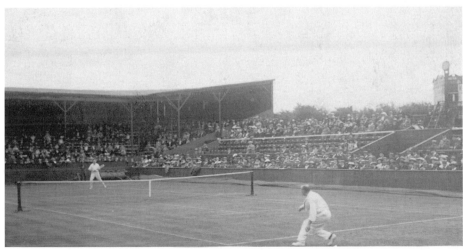

The centre court at the Worple Road grounds in 1913. The All England Croquet Club was founded in 1868 with lawns in Worple Road and to attract new members added the increasingly popular game of lawn tennis to its title in 1877. Featured here is the game between the Briton, Mr H. Roper Barrett and the American, Mr M.E. McLoughlin (who won 4–6, 8–6, 1–6, 6–2, 8–6; no tie breaks in those days).

The final in the gentlemen's singles in 1909. It was between M.J. Ritchie and A.W. Gore, who became men's champion by winning 6–8, 1–6, 6–2, 6–2, 6–2.

Tennis match between Mrs E. Thompson and Mrs D. Douglas, 1908 or 1909. Mrs Douglas was champion seven times. The Worple Road grounds were becoming too crowded and the decision was made to move to Wimbledon Park. The old grounds were taken over by the High School in 1923, which used them for a hockey pitch together with three hard and four grass tennis courts.

Section Six

PEOPLE &
BUILDINGS

*St Mary's Parish Church, c. 1908. The church is probably that mentioned in
Domesday Book as belonging to the Manor of Wimbledon. Additions were made throughout
the seventeenth and eighteenth centuries; the structure we know today was built in 1843. Sir
Edward Cecil, Lord of the Manor, who died 16 November 1638, is buried in the family
vault within the church.*

Jack and Tiny, *c.* 1920. A charitable group named Our Dumb Friends League kept a trace horse called Jack at the bottom of Wimbledon Hill to assist horse-drawn vehicles pulling their loads up the hill. A set of charges was listed that rose to one shilling. Tiny the little pony pulling a 'horse ambulance' was used as a collector to draw in the funds and could also be seen on Putney Hill and Kingston Hill.

Wimbledon theatre in the Broadway, *c.* 1914. It was opened in 1910 with, appropriately, a pantomime, productions for which it is well known. Many West End plays have had their first airing on the large stage here.

Wimbledon from the air in 1920. The old tennis grounds in Worple Road can be seen top right. Middle left is St John's Church on the junction with Spencer Hill. Murray Road, Denmark Road and Thornton Road can be seen leading away from The Ridgway at the bottom.

Wimbledon from the air in 1920. Worple Road is to the lower end of this view and the white Church of the Sacred Heart on Edge Hill is in the centre. The Rushmere pond and common with Southside and Westside is to the top.

Ecclesbourne High School for Boys, 24 Worple Road, in 1908. The principal, William Layton, administered to boys over the age of seven years old who were taught a complete range of subjects, including a variety of modern languages, particularly Spanish and French. Boarders were taken, but limited to twelve living on the premises.

The Paragon Press, also called the Merton Printing Works, in 1920. It was situated at 138 Merton Road between Ridley Road and Quicks Road; the staff are standing proudly outside. The notice in the window is for a football match on Saturday 6 March 1920 at the John Innes ground, Cannon Hill Lane, Merton, between Merton and Oxford University Centaurs, and adds 'Support your local hospital'.

St Luke's Church, Farquhar Road, Wimbledon Park, *c.* 1910. The church was erected in 1908–9 to the designs of T.G. Jackson RA, at a cost of £15,000. Seating for 800 was provided and the living was held by the Revd William John Williamson MA of University College, Durham.

South Park Gardens in 1910; then as now a welcome retreat for those living in neighbouring Trinity Road, Dudley Road and King's Road.

The school in Queen's Road, *c.* 1912. It was built in 1902 and enlarged in 1904 to accommodate 546 boys, 546 girls and 637 infants. Although the average attendance for boys crept up to 585, that for girls was only 488. The school still rings to the sounds of eager learners.

Wimbledon High School, *c.* 1906. It was founded in 1880. The old building in Mansell Road was destroyed by fire in 1917; the rebuilding in 1920 added a reference library, some very fine studios, a gymnasium and three laboratories. In 1923 the old lawn tennis grounds in Worple Road were acquired. The school is still going strong.

The Broadway, *c.* 1926. The large three-storey building was Holy Trinity Council School until it was partially converted in 1910 for use as the King's Palace cinema. The building also contained the Temperance billiard hall, and a roller skating rink was in operation during the 1920s somewhere within the structure. After the cinema closed on 30 April 1955, the building was used as a shopping arcade. The complex was demolished in the early 1990s and as of April 1995 the site is awaiting redevelopment.

St Winifred's Catholic Church, Merton Road, *c.* 1910. Designed by Frederick A. Walters FSA in the Romanesque style, the church was built in 1904–5 at a cost of £6,500.

The Clevelands Hotel, 99 Church Road, in 1935. It was one of many large houses converted to hotel use between the two wars. The hotel's proprietors were Major Clement Hertzel OBE and Mrs Hertzel.

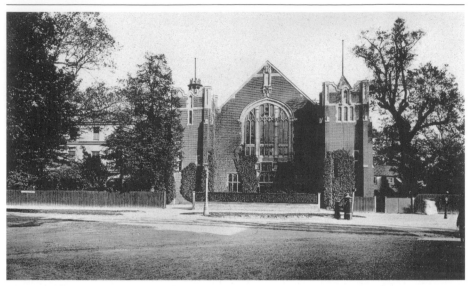

King's College School, Southside, *c*. 1912. The school moved to Wimbledon in 1897 and has maintained a high degree of excellence with many pupils going on to university. Sport has always been an important part of the curriculum, and below we see boys playing cricket in the school grounds.

Pelham Road School, *c.* 1910. It was built to accommodate 352 boys, 352 girls and 362 infants. The headmaster in 1920 was Mr A.E. Hill, the headmistress Miss A. Gomm and the infants' mistress Miss M. Reed. Pelham was the Christian name of a developer in the area.

The Wimbledon and District Foot Hospital, 68 Merton High Street, in the 1930s. Situated fifty yards from South Wimbledon station, its well-equipped cubicles are clearly visible.

A hand-pushed dairy cart of the North Hants Dairy Co., 27 the Broadway, *c.* 1910. The milk was drawn from the large churn and delivered to each household in the measured cans hanging from the upper rail. Due to the lack of refrigeration, deliveries were two and sometimes three times a day to the larger households.

B. Turvey of Wimbledon, *c.* 1910. The delivery man is standing proudly by his steed turned out in almost showground condition. The firm must have been short lived as it does not appear in local directories, but the possibility exists that a Benjamin Turvey at No. 13 the Ridgway, listed from 1905 to 1913, may be the same as in the photograph. The firm was either a bakery, laundry or a transport company, according to the basket on the tailgate.

District Railway engine No. 4, *c.* 1905. The train was in service on the underground line to Wimbledon between 1889 and 1905 when the line was electrified. The tubes across the engine were part of a system that consumed the smoke while the train was within tunnels.

Train crash, Wimbledon station, 27 June 1927. A six-coach District Line train, entering platform No. 2, was on the crossover when it was hit by a four-coach train leaving platform No. 3. Eight people were injured, suffering mainly from broken legs and chest injuries. The line was blocked for the rest of the day which caused some confusion during the height of the Wimbledon tennis championships. The ambulance housed at Queen's Road fire station dashed to the scene, scattering waiting passengers. Splinters of wood and pieces of iron could be seen on the track the next day.

The Atkinson Morley Hospital. It was founded in 1869 as a convalescent hospital for St George's Hospital at Hyde Park. In the photograph above we see nurses and patients taking the air on the veranda, *c.* 1922. The earlier picture below, taken before the First World War, is of some cows at the hospital, probably kept to supply fresh milk.

Height: 175 Ft.
Internal } 11 Ft.
Diameter

Wimbledon Corporation electricity works at Durnsford Road, *c.* 1910. The chimney, 175 ft tall, was built in 1899 by Alphons Custodis Chimney Construction Co. of Victoria Street, Westminster. Plant capacity in 1910 was 3,685 kw and by 1925 was increased to 10,125 kw, with 8,570,130 units of electricity sold at the rates of 4½*d* per unit for lighting, 1*d* per unit for heating and cooking and 1¾*d* per unit for power. The plant and buildings were removed during the 1970s and the site is now a small electricity substation and a DIY store.

Queen Alexandra's Court, Woodside Road and St Mary's Road. It was founded in 1899 by Colonel Sir James Gildea KCVO, CB as a home for officers' widows and daughters. The building was opened on 15 July 1905 by King Edward VII and Queen Alexandra, who gave £5,000 towards the costs. The aerial view is of *c.* 1920 and the scene below at the junction of St Mary's Road and Woodside Road is of *c.* 1910.

The Queen's House, Church Hill, *c.* 1910. It was purchased together with 1½ acres of land in 1908 and adapted to contain three apartments for ladies as an addition to Queen Alexandra's Court. Before the First World War, the ground staff comprised (from the left in the photograph below) the head gardener, three gardeners and the superintendent; they pose for the camera with the tools of their trade.

The petrol pumps and forecourt of Benton Roberts motor engineers, 614 Garratt Lane, Summerstown, on the corner of Maskell Road, *c.* 1930. The pump prices are Redline Super 1*s* 2½*d*, Redline Benzol mixture 1*s* 2½*d* and the Redline Commercial 1*s* ½*d* per gallon. These prices were unchanged from 1903 until 1932 when premium grades were increased to 1*s* 4*d*.

The tank *Egbert* on display outside the town hall, 14 March 1918. Its purpose was to encourage the purchase of war bonds. Five tanks were displayed across the country and the local mayors, the military and boy scouts would attend the displays.

King Edward VII and Queen Alexandra driving along the High Street in an open carriage on Saturday 15 July 1905 to open Queen Alexandra's Court (see pp. 74–5).

The Nelson Hospital on the Kingston Road, *c.* 1926. The hospital was built in 1911 at a cost of £32,000 and opened in 1912. As a memorial to the men who fell in the First World War, the Borough of Merton added a new wing in 1922, with a commemorative plaque above the entrance.

The Wimbledon Hospital on Copse Hill, *c*. 1914. It was erected in 1869 as a cottage hospital. This smaller hospital was demolished and rebuilt at a cost of £10,000, reopening in 1912 with accommodation for thirty-two patients. The Nurses' Home, seen below *c*. 1924, was opened in May 1922 by Field Marshal Earl Haig. The hospital, declared redundant in the 1980s, has been demolished and the land sold for housing.

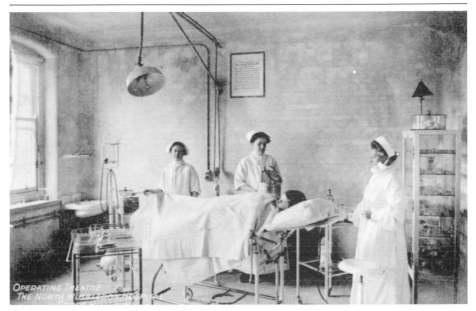

A patient on the trolley awaits his operation in the well-equipped operating theatre at Wimbledon Hospital, early 1920s.

The Church of the Sacred Heart on Edge Hill, c. 1912. It was built between 1887 and 1899 at a cost of £33,000 exclusive of the ground and internal fittings. Designed by Frederick A. Walters FSA, the church has impressive dimensions: the nave is 58 ft tall and 78 ft wide and the church is nearly 200 ft long.

Wimbledon Stadium, Plough Road, *c.* 1960. Greyhound racing was the original sport held here; later the cinder track was made available for motor cycle speedway races and more recently used for stock car racing.

The Woodman public house, Durnsford Road, *c.* 1924. The pub was built in 1898 when the surrounding area was still farmland and its only neighbour was the railway line alongside. The bus to King's Cross is waiting for a change of crew.

WIMBLEDON
STREETS

Alan Road, c. 1910. The road is situated on the former site of the lawns of Belvedere
House, which was demolished at the beginning of the twentieth century.

Alexandra Road, *c.* 1912. A late Victorian development of former market gardens and open fields alongside the railway. The magistrates' court was rebuilt on the railway side during the 1980s. The road is probably named after Princess Alexandra, later the Princess of Wales, wife of King Edward VII.

Alverstone Avenue, *c.* 1912. Between Revelstoke Road and Ashen Grove, this was part of the Edwardian housing development instigated by Mr John Beaumont in the mid-nineteenth century, in the Southfields area. Alverstone is a small village on the Isle of Wight.

Arthur Road, *c*. 1912. The 'Arthur' was the Duke of Connaught, third son of Queen Victoria, who held various important military positions. The road was laid out by 1878 but this shopping parade was not added until 1906.

Arthur Road in 1907, with Wimbledon Park station on the left. The shops lower down the road had just been built and the children could still walk in the roads without the worry of speeding traffic.

The recently electrified District Line at Wimbledon Park station in 1907. A High Street Kensington train is on the up platform. The station was opened in 1889.

Arthur Road in 1908. St Mary's Parish Church is nearby; the large trees overhanging the road evoke the atmosphere of rural Surrey.

Avondale Road, *c.* 1914. It lies between Gap Road and Cromwell Road. The only traffic to be seen is one hand-pushed delivery cart and one horse-drawn van. The eldest son of King Edward VII was Duke of Clarence and Avondale, a parish in Lanarkshire.

Burghley Road, *c.* 1910. In 1536 Lord Cecil Burghley became Lord of the Manor. He was secretary to Lord Protector Somerset and an influential statesman under Edward VI and Queen Mary.

Copse Hill in 1906. At the time the lane was still not much more than an agricultural pathway to Cottenham Park.

Courtney Gardens, *c.* 1906. The road surface is rather muddy and rutted, so the photograph was probably taken either before development was complete or before the road was properly laid down. The gardens were renamed Dora Road in 1906/7.

Dryden Road, *c.* 1912. Looking down from Haydon's Road, across the Wandle to the Grove Hospital at Tooting, now St George's Hospital. The roads hereabouts are named after English writers – John Dryden (1631–1700) was one of our most prolific poets and a popular dramatist.

Durnsford Avenue, *c.* 1930. The owner of a bullnose Morris motor car in the 1930s had plenty of space in which to park his vehicle. Development commenced in this road in 1906.

Edge Hill, *c.* 1910. Originally just a fieldway between the Ridgway and Worple Road, the road was developed in the 1860s and 1880s with several large houses for families who could afford to employ several servants. In the 1960s and '70s many of these fine houses were demolished and small blocks of flats erected.

Gap Road, *c.* 1912. On the right is the Wimbledon Isolation Hospital for Infectious Diseases which opened in 1900. It covered five acres, contained eighty-two beds and was built at a cost of £21,000. The hospital has since been demolished and council housing erected. In 1866 this was known as Garratt Road but was renamed to avoid confusion with Garratt Lane. The Garratt was a small cluster of cottages near Earlsfield police station. On a map of 1890 the road from the railway bridge to Plough Lane was called Cemetery Road; understandably this was soon changed.

Hamilton Road in 1906. This road is on a small grid of streets off Merton High Street that has a Nelson connection. Lady Emma Lyon Hamilton (1761–1815), wife of Sir William Hamilton, British ambassador at Naples, is best known for her association with Admiral Nelson. She bought land in Merton in 1801 (see p. 93).

Hartfield Road, *c.* 1914. S. Love and Son ironmongers could display an array of their wares on the pavement probably without the worry of theft. In 1865 the road was partially a field path leading to the White Hart Inn, where Nelson's Merton property was auctioned in 1823.

Haydon's Road with a newly introduced tram en route to Summerstown via Plough Road in 1906 (above), and with little girls, *c.* 1910 (below). The girls pose safely for the camera in the roadway, some of them clutching dolls. In the background is the Horse and Groom public house. Frank Haydon and his wife Ellen Rayne, of West Barnes, lived at Southey Lodge in Southey Road near the Broadway in the 1860s, although Haydons are recorded locally from Tudor times.

Home Park Road, *c.* 1910. This part of the road was developed before the Council sold off a portion of its Wimbledon Park purchase (see p. 53).

Leopold Road, *c.* 1907. The part of this road from Alexandra Road to Gap railway bridge was originally known as Gap Road but renamed as part of Leopold Road. Queen Victoria's fourth son was Leopold, Duke of Albany (1853–84).

Melrose Avenue, *c.* 1910. The Arthur Road estate agents, Ryan and Penfold, requested the name change from Elsenham Road, and this was granted in 1905/6. Daniel Rucker renamed his house Melrose Hall, in West Hill, Wandsworth, after Melrose Abbey where he spent his honeymoon. Melrose Hall is now the Home for Incurables.

Murray Road, *c.* 1910. The British Land Co. developed the area in 1906/7 and named the road after General Sir Henry Murray, the owner of Wimbledon Lodge which stood on the site.

Nelson Road in 1906. In 1801 Lady Hamilton purchased 70 acres of farmland in Merton as a home for Admiral Horatio Nelson. The estate was bounded by Quicks Road and Merton Road on the west and Haydon's Road on the east, with the house where Nelson Grove is now.

Normanton Avenue, c. 1912. Clonmore Road in Southfields where building commenced between 1896 and 1901 originally extended to Ashen Grove but this section to Revelstoke Road was renamed Normanton Avenue as announced by the Council on 27 November 1906.

Queen's Road, near the junction with Haydon's Road, *c.* 1912. Queen's Road school on the corner of Craven Gardens can be seen further down on the right.

Somerset Road, *c.* 1910. At this date it was still a gravel-laid trackway. The Duke of Somerset was resident at the manor house from 1827 and in 1838 Queen Victoria was entertained there. The Duchess of Somerset was a benefactor of the almshouses on Westside.

Strathearne Road, c. 1908. The road was laid out by 1882 and housing development followed soon after. Queen Victoria's father was Edward Augustus (1767–1820), Duke of Kent and Strathearne, fourth son of King George III.

Woodside Parade in Leopold Road, c. 1912. Walker's Dairy can be seen in the middle of this row of shops which then, as now, is full of delivery vehicles.

Woodside Road, *c.* 1912. On the 1890 Ordnance Survey map the only properties were Lismore, Abbotsford and Woodside Lodge and the large nursery at the Hill Road end.

Wyclife Road, *c.* 1907. Most side roads could be safely used by the young boys in the area for their games, which included cricket and football. Boots and knickerbockers together with celluloid collars were part of every boy's dress.

RAYNES PARK

The Kingston Road, c. 1912. At this time this parade of shops included the receiving office for the Magnet Laundry, Henry Hill bootmaker, Arthur Wyatt's coffee shop and the oil shop of George Field.

The Kingston Road, *c.* 1925. On the corner of Russell Road, on the right, is William Wood's off licence (No. 141); at No. 143 is the cycle dealer William Wilcox and at No. 147 is Arthur Ashby's dairy. On the left at No. 136 is J.W. Welch's bakery and post office.

Merton Park level crossing in 1920. The White Hart public house, probably an eighteenth-century inn, has since been rebuilt. The White Hart motor garage, now demolished, had various cars for hire; the proprietor was Mr H. White.

Merton Park level crossing in 1907. The station at Merton Park, called Lower Merton until 1877 and then renamed, was opened in 1857/8; the rail line from Wimbledon to Croydon commenced operations in 1855. The level crossing saved installing a road bridge and the demolition of the White Hart.

Corner of Merton Hall Road and Kingston Road in 1908. The grocer's shop of Gurney Mason is on the corner (No. 156). The parade included a butcher's, chemist's, dairy, draper's, boot stores and a hardware shop.

The Kingston Road at Raynes Park, *c.* 1926. The Salvation Army hut on the corner of Sydney Road is now used by them as a local community hall and called The Bash. At No. 406, next door, was Morgan's Dairy and at No. 404 Frank Battalion's confectionary shop. The picture below shows the houses opposite. Chestnut Road is opposite these properties.

The parade of shops in the Kingston Road opposite Raynes Park station, *c.* 1910. The skew bridge (see below) is in the background. The grocers of the time traded in coal and coke, as you can see from the shop on the left. Even the little dog is looking at the camera.

The original route for the Kingston Road, *c.* 1908, with the skew bridge for the railway at Raynes Park station. The road was relegated to pedestrian use when a straight roadway a few yards away was installed in 1973.

Worple Road, Cottenham Park, *c.* 1914. The Raynes Park Laundry site on the left is now occupied by a petrol station. The Methodist church on the corner of Tolverne Road was opened for worship in March 1914. Built in the Byzantine style, it had seating for 650. The original church of corrugated iron was replaced by Bond Hall whose foundation stone was laid on 18 June 1927 by George Heaver. The opening ceremony is seen in the lower view. Bond Hall is named after William Samuel Bond, superintendent for thirty-five years (1893–1928).

Two views of the Raynes Park Hotel in 1907. It was rebuilt in 1904. It is now better known as a major public house, the Raynes Park Tavern. The Raync family owned the West Barncs Park estate until 1866 when it was sold to Richard Garth; he paid £4,000 for the station to be built, which opened in 1871.

Raynes Park, *c.* 1910. Before the Bushey Road dual carriageway was built in 1927, to connect with the Kingston bypass, this road and West Barnes Lane were the main routes to and from west Wimbledon. Ground-floor extensions to the shops on the left of the public house have altered the parade's appearance.

Coombe Lane at the corner of Amity Grove, *c.* 1908. West Barnes Lane is a little further to the left. Some of the larger houses on the right are dated 1879, when the attached gardens still fronted the roadside. These have gradually given way to shops and semi-detached houses.

Coombe Lane in 1907 (above) and 1910 (below). The open tributary of the Pyll brook is fenced in beside the roadway. When the Malden section of Coombe Lane was renamed Coombe Lane West in 1961, there was an unsuccessful proposal to rename this part Coombe Lane East.

Mr J.E. White's hairdresser's and tobacconist's shop, No. 484 Kingston Road, *c.* 1910.
Besides the many brands of tobacco on display is a variety of men's toiletry accessories.

Two delivery carts of the Stone Farm Dairy, based at No. 528 Kingston Road, *c.* 1910. The photograph was not taken in high summer, for then the highly polished churns would have had a cloth insulation blanket fitted over them.

Amity Grove, *c.* 1910. The land was bought in 1868 by the Amity Investment Company and developed *c.* 1880 by the Amity Trust.

Bronson Road, *c.* 1912. Development here had started by 1901. This road is known as one of the 'twelve apostles', a local nickname which was chosen because there are twelve similar streets in the area.

Cambridge Road, *c.* 1914. Named after George, Duke of Cambridge who owned land in the area in the 1830s. The larger houses in this road were home to such people as Thomas C. Summerhay, a local justice of the peace (No. 1), and A.W. Hughes, the honorary secretary of the Cottenham Park Civic Association (No. 45).

Carlton Park Avenue, *c.* 1910. Bakeries had their own horse vans to deliver bread, a service that died out with the advent of supermarkets. Before the Second World War the majority of married women were at home to receive deliveries.

Chestnut Road, *c.* 1910. The delivery van is from Follet & Sons bakers of Wimbledon Broadway. Mr Charles Bertie Jackson-Willis, who resided at No. 18 after the First World War, was the secretary to the National Deposit Friendly Society.

A new house for sale in Church Walk during the late 1920s. Cannon Hill Estates Ltd were offering these semi-detached properties at £910 freehold with a ground rent of £9 10s.

Clifton Park Avenue, *c.* 1910. In 1925 the local window cleaning was provided by the Raynes Park & District Window Cleaning Service from premises at No. 57.

Cottenham Park Road, *c.* 1912. In 1920 Major Alexander Robinson resided at No. 23 and William Ward, solicitor and commisioner for oaths, lived at No. 27.

Dorien Road, *c.* 1910. On the west side at No. 5 was the London City Mission hall with Mr W. Martin as preacher. The two boys seem to have followed the cameraman around the local roads as he took a series of photographs on the same day – see the views of Edna Road (p. 114) and Vernon Avenue (p. 122).

Dunmore Road, *c.* 1912. Development here started in 1907, but the street was then named Commondale Road. It was renamed after Dunmore House.

Durham Road, *c.* 1912. In the background (above) is St Matthew's Church, originally opening in a corrugated iron building in 1892. The permanent church, seen here, had seating for 400 and had cost £4,000 by 1915. George Lampton, Earl of Durham, owned much of the land hereabouts (see p. 118). Monsieur H.J.B. Passat, who moved to No. 106 *c.* 1907, was firmly wedded to the ornithopter, a flapping-wing aeroplane. By 1910 he had produced an aircraft with a wing span of 24 ft, operated by a system of gears and levers and powered by a 4.5 h.p. motor cycle engine, the machine having a bird-like appearance. Passat tested the design on Wimbledon Common and after flying for a distance of 150 yd 'his passage was arrested by a tree'. In 1912 he made more attempts to fly and in 1919 he even persuaded the RAF to test one of his designs.

Durham Flats, *c.* 1906. This was a series of flats with double-door entrances – one for the ground-floor flat and one for the flat on the first floor. They were situated on the corner of Durham Road and Cambridge Road.

Edna Road, *c.* 1910. Another of the 'twelve apostles' with the same two boys again appearing for the camera.

Two houses in Fairway for sale in 1927. The agents were again Cannon Hill Estates Ltd, and the price was £685 freehold, £10 down and £65 on completion, with the balance paid as rent at 22*s* 7*d* per week. The houses contained 1,050 sq. ft of floor space and boasted three bedrooms, two reception rooms, bathroom, separate WC and two hot-water geysers.

Prince George's Avenue, *c*. 1910. The Raynes Park Conservative & Unionist Club was here; in 1925 J.B. Owen was the honorary secretary and J.M. Edwards the resident steward.

Gore Road, *c*. 1912. This delivery cart had travelled some distance, as the firm is Hudson Brothers provision merchants of Ludgate Hill in London EC.

The golf house in 1907. The Raynes Park golf club was founded in 1893 and had over 400 members by 1924. The grounds are now covered over by Fairway, Linkway and Greenway Roads, the golfing connection surviving in the names.

Grand Drive, *c.* 1922. The open parkland of the golf links is seen shortly before development was to cover the area with bricks and mortar.

The area around Grand Drive with open parkland on the right beyond the trees down to the Kingston Road and Raynes Park in 1907. St Saviour's Church is on the left just beyond the trees.

Semi-detached properties for sale in Grand Drive, *c.* 1928. Canon Hill Estates Ltd were advertising them at £860 freehold, £25 down payment and £75 on completion. Unusually, space was available for a garage.

A parade of shops in Lambton Road, near Coombe Road, in 1914. The newspaper placards at F. Woodfield's newsagents are reporting 'Serbian Panic' and 'Belgrade Occupied'. The off-licence at No. 16 on the corner belonged to F. Leney & Co.; the mosaic in the entrance still reads F. Leney and the shop is still an off-licence.

Lambton Road, *c.* 1910. The Cottenham Park Estate was owned in 1825–31 by George Lambton, Earl of Durham (1792–1840). He was instrumental in resolving administrative grievances in Canada in 1838, a process that led to the country's self-government in 1867. Development of Lambton Road was largely completed by 1907.

Melbury Gardens in 1925. Residents here included, at No. 56, Captain Reginald Byrne, OBE, MC; at No. 58, Lady Constance Monro; at No. 60, Lady Fry; at No. 78, Thomas F. Griffin MD, DPH; and at No. 80, on the corner of Laurel Grove, Horace X. Brown, Surgeon General.

Pepys Road, *c.* 1910. The road was laid out in the 1850s and was named after Charles Pepys, an owner of much land in the area.

Richmond Road, which was named after the Duke of Richmond, *c.* 1926. Many local societies were maintained in the area after the First World War, and the West Wimbledon Society with T.E. Jenner as chairman used the Avenue Road Hall for its meetings. On the next corner at No. 64 lived Captain William Beamish Robert de la Cour.

St Saviour's Church, Grand Drive, *c.* 1910. The foundation stone was laid on 22 July 1905 by Sir Frederick Wigan Bt., five years after the creation of the St Saviour Mission in a small tin hut that became the boys' hall after the church opened in 1907. A stone war memorial was placed in front of the church after the First World War; by 1995 nearly all of the names have worn away.

Sydney Road, *c.* 1910. This road was home to the artisans of the district, and in 1925 we have at No. 48, Alfred Penny gardener; at No. 80, James Ford decorator; and at No. 84, S.F. Petitt bootmaker.

Tolverne Road, *c.* 1925. Supposedly one of the roads in the area with a Cornish connection; many villages in Cornwall have Tol in their name, but a Tolverne is not listed in any gazetteer of British town names.

Vernon Avenue, *c.* 1910. This road is among the twelve leading off the Kingston Road to the east of Raynes Park station which have the local nickname of 'the twelve apostles'.

Holland Gardens, *c.* 1933. A plaque on the gate of the gardens bears the following inscription: This land was given by Lady Holland of 'Holmhurst' Wimbledon and her family as an open space for the use and enjoyment of the public and was named 'Holland Gardens' in commemoration of the beneficent and public services of the late Sir Arthur Holland JP during his long residence in Wimbledon. Opened July 1929. Much of the gardens were taken up for use as air raid shelters during the Second World War.

Bradbury Wilkinson's works, *c.* 1924. Security printers of banknotes and postage stamps, the firm moved from the City to Burlington Road on a 15 acre site in 1921. Many locals found full- and part-time employment at this and other factories near Shannons Corner. The building was demolished and a Tesco food supermarket opened on the site in 1987.

Carter's seed company, *c.* 1910. The firm was founded in 1837 by James Carter with premises in Holborn and nurseries at Forest Hill. In 1909 it purchased 19 acres of land in West Barnes and by 1910 had constructed the main building seen here. The following years saw further expansion with laboratories and storage sheds being erected. The site was sold to the local council in 1967 and a housing estate now covers the old grounds and factory.

The level crossing at West Barnes Lane, *c.* 1926. This was originally installed in 1859 during the construction of the Wimbledon-to-Dorking railway. The crossing served as an access road to the West Barnes estate of the Rayne family. A crossing keeper is no longer required as the gates are automatically closed when a train approaches.

West Barnes Lane, near the level crossing, in 1907. The London United Tramways service to Kingston and Hampton Court had to pass through a landscape of wilderness for some years, before development caught up with the area.

Broadwater Farm, *c.* 1905. In 1871 the farm consisted of 180 acres between Cannon Hill Lane to the west and the Kingston Road. William Rayne bought the farm to add to his holding in the vicinity, growing crops which included beans, cabbage, hay and wheat; he also kept cattle, pigs and horses, the last being used for ploughing and carting. The farm became a dairy farm in 1901 and supplied milk to Wimbledon and district. After the First World War the farm was broken up and the Whatley housing estate built.

Wooden stile across a ditch in the vicinity of Whatley Avenue, *c.* 1912. The railway embankment leading to Wimbledon Chase railway station is in the background.

The view from Kingston Road across the fields and a stream, looking towards Raynes Park School, *c.* 1912.

Raynes Park School, *c.* 1912. The school was built in 1909 to accommodate 350 boys, 350 girls and 340 infants. It was later renamed the Joseph Hood School and in 1985 became Merton Adult Education Centre.

BRITAIN IN OLD PHOTOGRAPHS